WILDLIFE IN BLOOM SERIES

Little Bobcat

BY AUTHOR & CONSERVATIONIST

LINDA BLACKMOOR

ISBN: 978-1-966417-04-0 (PRINT)

PUBLISHED BY QUILL PRESS. LINDA BLACKMOOR'S TITLES MAY BE
PURCHASED IN BULK FOR EDUCATIONAL, BUSINESS, FUNDRAISING, OR
SALES PROMOTIONAL USE. FOR INFORMATION, PLEASE EMAIL
HELLO@LINDABLACKMOOR.COM

FIRST PRINT EDITION: 2024

LINDA BLACKMOOR
WWW.LINDABLACKMOOR.COM

SPECIES

Bobcats are wild cats native to North America, found from southern Canada through the U.S. to northern Mexico. They are named for their short, "bobbed" tails, which are about 6 inches long. Weighing between 15 and 35 pounds and measuring up to 4 feet in length, bobcats are about twice the size of domestic cats. They belong to the Felidae family and are closely related to other species like the lynx.

LOOKS

Bobcats have tufted ears, spotted coats, and whiskered faces that give them a uniquely distinct look. Their fur ranges from light gray to reddish-brown, adorned with dark spots and streaks that help them blend into their surroundings. The ear tufts enhance their hearing, while their keen eyes provide excellent night vision. Their large, padded paws enable silent movement in their habitats.

BOBCAT FACT #3

HABITAT

These adaptable creatures thrive in a variety of habitats, including forests, deserts, swamps, and even suburban areas. Bobcats prefer regions with dense vegetation for cover and abundant prey to hunt. They are the most widely distributed wild cat in North America, found throughout the United States. Their ability to survive in both hot and cold climates showcases their remarkable adaptability.

BOBCAT FACT #4

DIET

As carnivores, bobcats primarily feast on small animals like rabbits, hares, rodents, birds, and insects. They are opportunistic hunters and occasionally prey on deer, especially fawns or injured individuals. By controlling rodent populations, bobcats play a vital role in maintaining ecological balance. They require about 2 to 3 pounds (0.9 to 1.4 kilograms) of meat daily to sustain themselves.

BOBCAT FACT #5

HUNTING

Bobcats are nocturnal hunters, relying on stealth and surprise to catch their prey under the cover of darkness. They have excellent hearing and vision, allowing them to detect prey in low-light conditions. Capable of leaping up to 10 feet (3 meters), they pounce on unsuspecting animals with precision. They stalk silently before making a swift, powerful attack.

ADAPT

Equipped with special adaptations, bobcats are effective predators in their environments. Their padded paws enable quiet movement, and retractable claws help them grip prey and climb trees. They possess a keen sense of smell and sharp teeth designed for slicing meat. Whiskers assist them in navigating the dark by sensing nearby objects.

KITTENS

Bobcats mate in late winter, and after a gestation period of about 60 to 70 days, the female gives birth to a litter of 2 to 4 kittens. Born blind and helpless, the kittens weigh around 10 to 12 ounces (283 to 340 grams). Their eyes open after about 10 days, and they stay with their mother for up to a year. During this time, she teaches them hunting skills and survival techniques.

TERRITORY

Bobcats are territorial animals, marking their ranges with scent and scratch marks on trees to communicate with others. A male's territory can cover up to 30 square miles and may overlap with the territories of several females. They are solitary creatures, typically coming together only during the mating season. Establishing territories helps reduce conflicts and competition for resources.

VOCAL

These wild cats communicate through various sounds like growls, hisses, snarls, and yowls. They may emit a chirping sound when excited or during mating season. Their vocalizations help them interact with other bobcats, especially for mating or territorial purposes. Body language, such as ear positioning and tail movements, also conveys their intentions and feelings.

LIFESPAN

In the wild, bobcats live an average of 7 to 10 years, but they can reach up to 16 years under ideal conditions. In captivity, with proper care, they may live over 20 years. Factors like predation, disease, and human-related dangers can affect their lifespan in the wild. While adult bobcats have few natural predators, they may fall prey to mountain lions, coyotes, or wolves.

BOBCAT FACT #11

PREDATOR

Young bobcat kittens are vulnerable to predators like owls, eagles, foxes, and even other bobcats. Human activities such as habitat destruction, hunting, and vehicle collisions pose significant threats to bobcat populations. Despite these challenges, bobcats are generally abundant due to their adaptability. They are classified as a species of Least Concern by the International Union for Conservation of Nature.

BOBCAT FACT #12

CAMO

The bobcat's spotted and striped fur provides excellent camouflage, allowing it to blend seamlessly into its environment. Their coat patterns mimic the dappled light of forests, hiding them from both prey and predators. This camo is essential for their hunting strategy, letting them approach prey undetected. Seasonal coat changes also help them adapt to different environments and climates.

BOBCAT FACT #13

SOLITARY

Bobcats are solitary animals, spending most of their lives alone except during mating season or when females are raising kittens. This solitary behavior reduces competition for food and resources within their territories. They are primarily crepuscular, being most active at dawn and dusk. Their independence requires them to be self-reliant and skilled hunters to survive.